Phillis Wheatley

Emily R. Smith, M.A.Ed.

Contributing Author

Wendy Conklin, M.A.

Publishing Credits

Rachelle Cracchiolo, M.S.Ed., *Publisher*
Conni Medina, M.A.Ed., *Managing Editor*
Emily R. Smith, M.A.Ed., *Series Developer*
Diana Kenney, M.A.Ed., NBCT, *Content Director*
Courtney Patterson, *Multimedia Designer*
Lynette Ordoñez, *Editor*

Image Credits: Cover, p. 1, 21, 27, 29 LOC [LC-USZC4-5316]; pp. 2–3 LOC [LC-USZC2-1465]; pp. 4, 5, 10, 16 Granger, NYC; p. 6 (back) LOC [LC-DIG-ppmsca-05933], (front) LOC [LC-USZ62-93962]; p. 7 LOC [LC-DIG-pga-05138]; p. 8 LOC [g8200.ct000124]; p. 9 LOC [bpe.28204300]; p. 11 LOC [gm71000622]; p. 12 LOC [LC-USZC4-772]; p. 13 (left) LOC [f0207s], The Library of Congress, (top) LOC [LC-USZ62-45506]; p. 14 LOC [LC-USZC2-1465]; pp. 13 (right), 15, 18, 21, 29, 32 The African American Odyssey Exhibition, The Library of Congress; p. 17 LOC [rbpe.0370260b]; pp. 19, 23, 28 North Wind Picture Archives; p. 19 (bottom right) Rare Book and Special Collections Division, The Library of Congress; p. 20 From the New York Public Library Digital Collections; p. 21 LOC [LC-USZ62-93956]; pp. 22, 31 Bridgeman Images; p. 24 LOC [0202001r]; p. 25 LOC [mgw3h/001/013012]; p. 25 LOC [LC-USZ62-102494]; p. 26 LOC [rbpe.1180320a]; pp. 19, back cover George Washington Papers at The Library of Congress, 1741-1799: Series 3h Varick Transcripts; all other images from iStock and/or Shutterstock.

Library of Congress Control Number: 2016939353

Teacher Created Materials
5301 Oceanus Drive
Huntington Beach, CA 92649-1030
http://www.tcmpub.com
ISBN 978-1-4938-3882-0

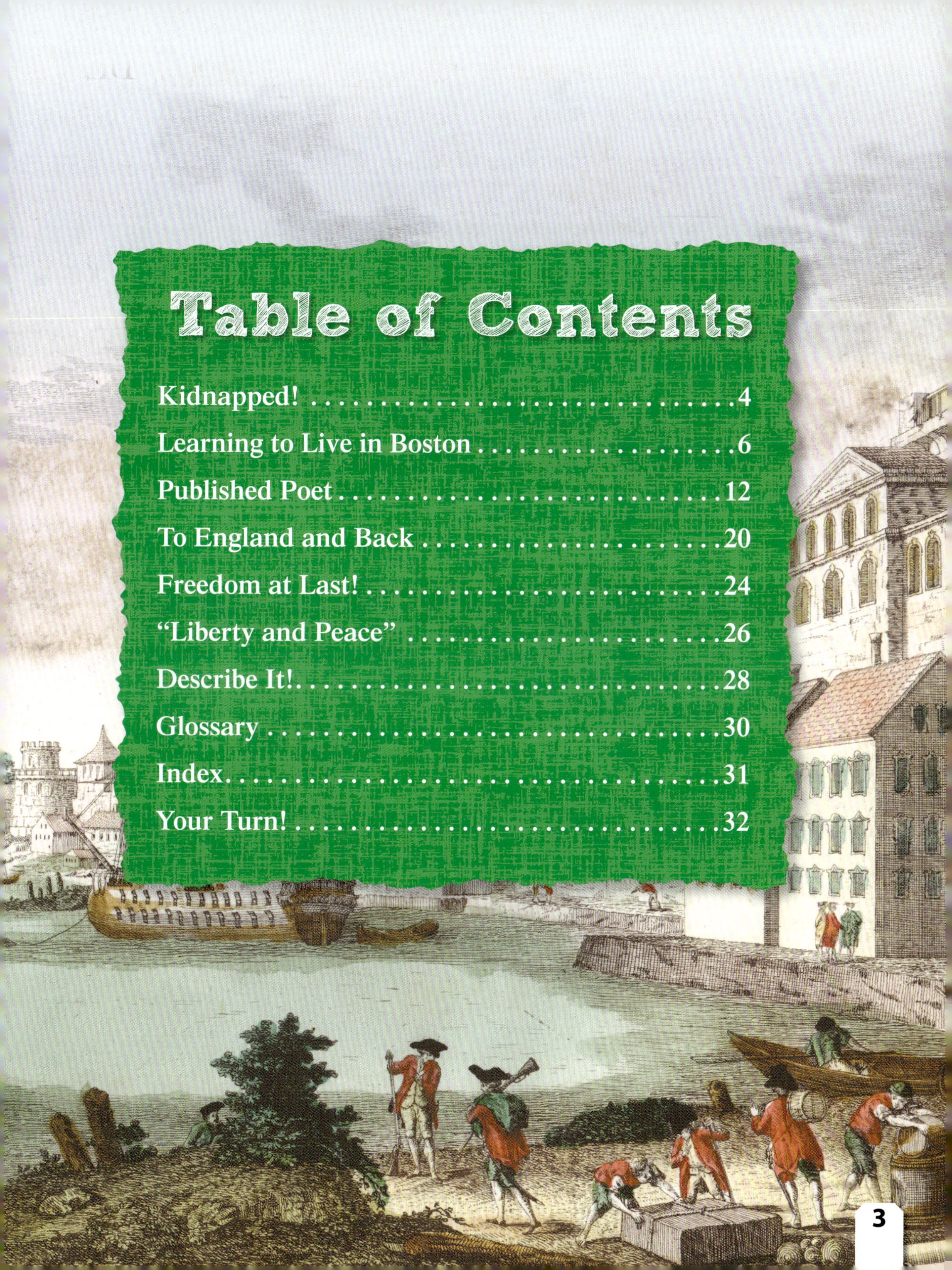

Table of Contents

Kidnapped!

When Phillis Wheatley was born in West Africa around 1753, she didn't know the life that was ahead of her. At the young age of seven, she was kidnapped by **slave** traders. They forced her onto a boat to Boston, Massachusetts. Phillis would soon be sold as a slave.

Phillis arrived in Boston in the summer of 1761. Boston looked very different from her homeland in Africa. Instead of grassy fields, Phillis saw a harbor filled with ships. People were busy making business deals. She had no idea how her life was about to change. It had already changed so much in the past 10 weeks at sea.

Slave traders take Africans to a ship.

The ship's owner needed to sell the slaves. And he wanted to sell them for top dollar. So, Phillis and the other slaves were cleaned and greased down to make them glisten in the sun. The men sold for a higher price because they looked like they could do more work. Phillis, on the other hand, was a small girl and looked weak in comparison. He priced her low in hopes of selling her quickly. Little did anyone know, she would become colonial America's first black female poet.

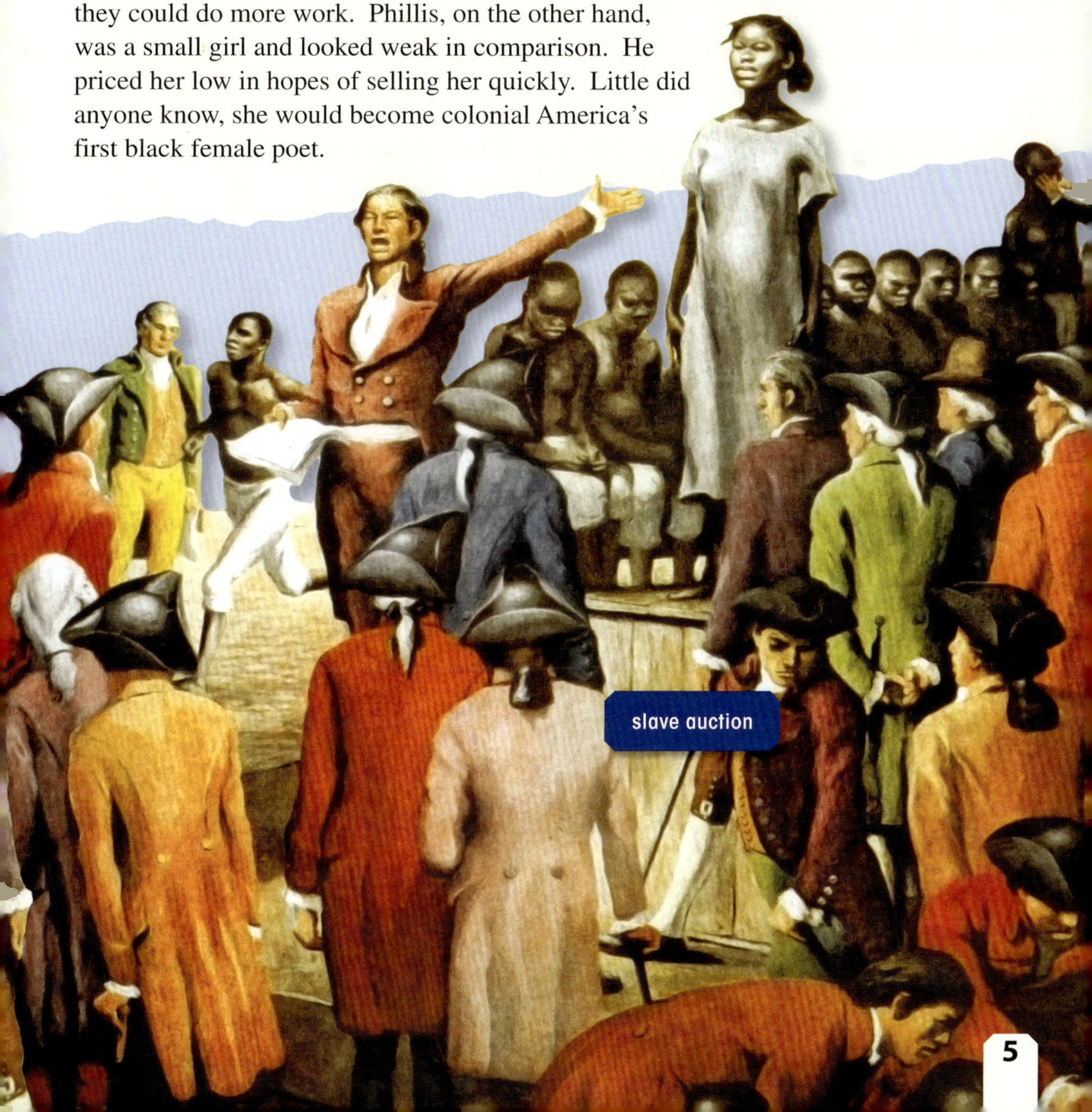

slave auction

Learning to Live in Boston

A wealthy Boston man named John Wheatley bought Phillis. He wanted her to be a servant for his wife, Susannah. John and Susannah named Phillis after the slave ship that brought her to the colonies. Her last name became Wheatley because they owned her.

Timothy Fitch

Timothy Fitch

A man named Timothy Fitch was a **slave merchant**. He traded molasses and rum for slaves in Africa. Then, he sold the slaves in America. Fitch owned the ship that brought Phillis to the colonies.

Slaves are held on a boat against their will.

The Wheatleys had two grown children. Their names were Mary and Nathaniel. Mary taught Phillis to read and write. Educating slaves was **illegal** in the southern colonies. But, in Boston, it was not against the law to teach a slave. That didn't mean people agreed with this. But, the Wheatleys could tell that Phillis was special.

Phillis enjoyed studying. The Bible was one of her favorite books. She learned to write by copying parts of the Bible. The people of Boston often saw her writing on fences or on the ground. She wrote with charcoal or sticks. Every new subject was exciting for Phillis.

Most slaves were from Africa. They didn't speak English. Slave traders took people from their homes and held them **captive** on overcrowded ships. Those ships spent weeks crossing the Atlantic Ocean. Can you imagine how scared they must have been?

The ships took the prisoners to the colonies. Most of them were brought to the southern colonies. Southern **plantation** owners wanted slaves as cheap labor. There were no plantations in the New England and middle colonies. So, fewer slaves were sold there.

In the South, there were laws that controlled what slaves could do. The laws were called *black codes*. The law against teaching slaves was an example of a black code. Black churchgoers were not allowed to go to the same churches as white churchgoers. These laws made the lives of slaves very hard.

map of Africa

Treatment of Slaves

Some slave owners treated their slaves poorly. They worked the slaves very hard and gave them little free time. Slaves were often beaten or punished. Most slave owners did not think of slaves as people. Instead, these men and women were considered property.

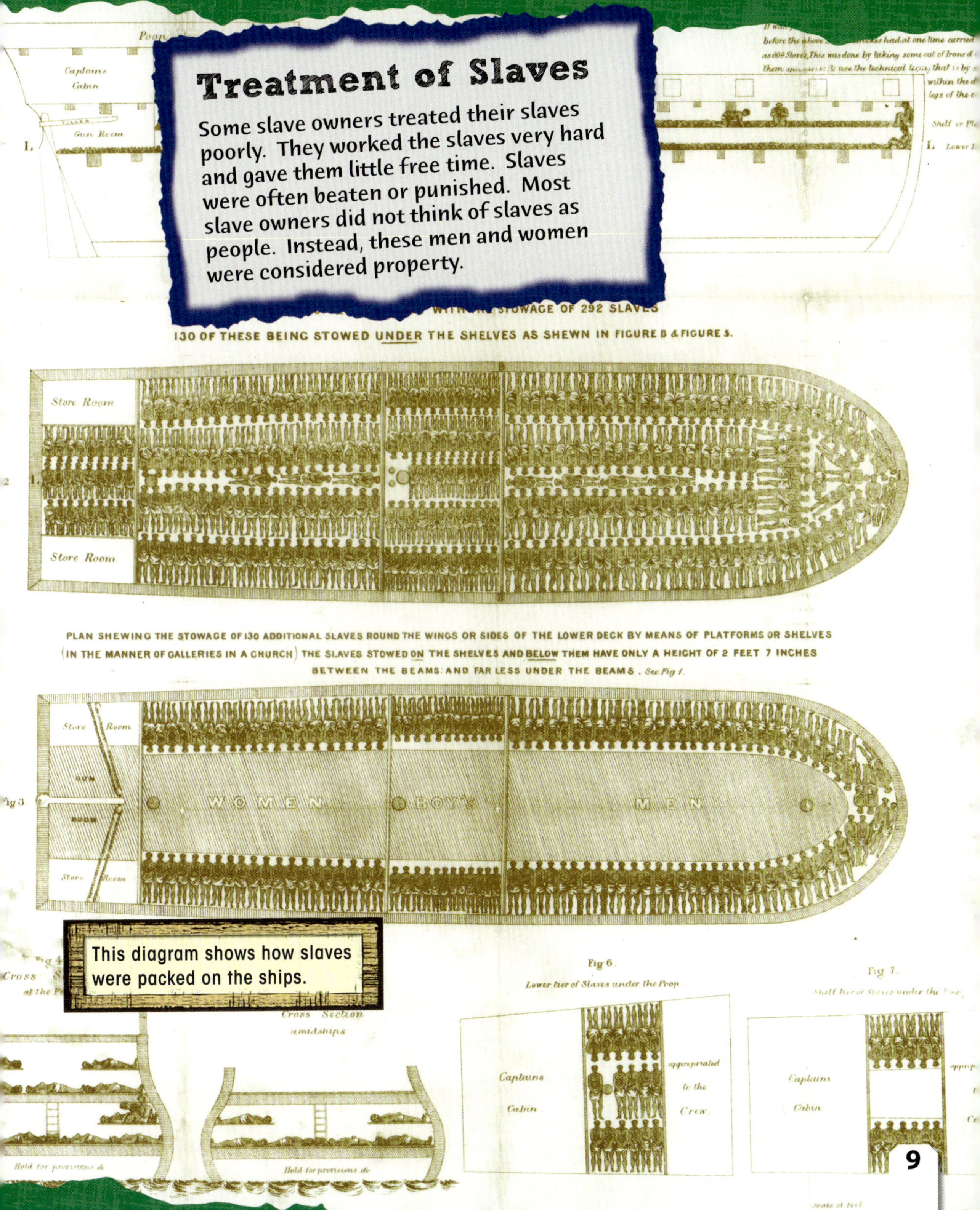

This diagram shows how slaves were packed on the ships.

The life of a slave was never easy. But, Phillis was luckier than most slaves. First of all, she lived in New England. Slaves in the North were usually treated better than slaves in the South. Most northern slaves were household servants. In the South, most of the slaves had to work in the fields all day. Working outside was harder on slaves' bodies than working inside.

In New England, slaves were allowed to go to "white" churches. But, they had to sit in separate areas. There were not as many laws in the North to control how people treated slaves.

Slaves pick cotton in the South.

map of Boston

The Wheatleys were kind to Phillis. They knew she was special and they helped her learn. Phillis once wrote that Mrs. Wheatley treated her "more like a child than her servant." Most slave owners did not treat their slaves like family.

In the end, Phillis was still a slave. She was not free to make her own choices or live her own life.

This is the only known image of Phillis created while she was alive.

Published Poet

Phillis was 14 when her first poem was published. She used poetry like a diary. She wrote about how she was feeling and what she was thinking. This was unusual for colonial poets. Most colonial poets did not share a lot of emotions in their poems.

Phillis also wrote about her emotions related to church. Religion was important to the Wheatley family. The Great Awakening took place in the 1730s and 1740s. This was a time when **ministers** tried to get more people to join their churches. Ministers traveled from town to town holding outdoor meetings. At these meetings, ministers helped people get excited about religion.

Alexander Pope

an outdoor religious meeting during the Great Awakening

Poetry Role Model

Phillis Wheatley was the first black woman in America to have her poetry published. That means she didn't have the chance to study poems by other black people. Instead, she learned by reading European poetry. Her favorite poet was Alexander Pope.

One minister that Phillis listened to at her church was George Whitefield. He was one of the most famous ministers from the Great Awakening. He was a great speaker. She enjoyed listening to Whitefield speak on Sundays. When he died, Phillis wrote a poem about him. The poem was published in Massachusetts and in England. This poem made her famous. She was just 17 years old.

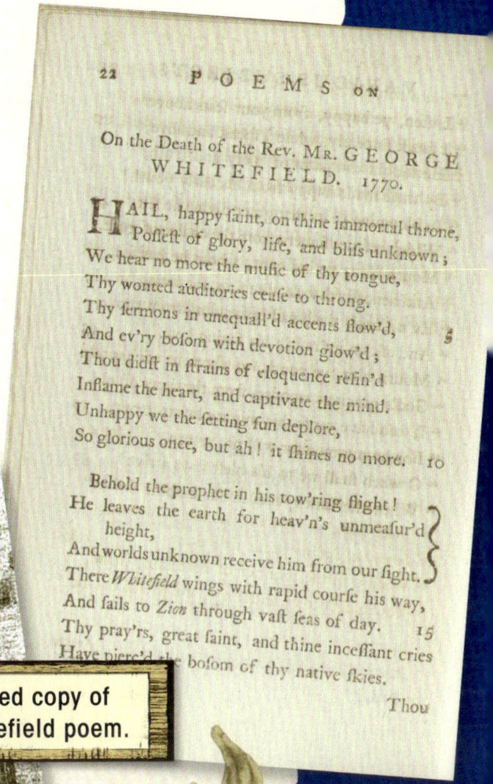
22 POEMS ON

On the Death of the Rev. MR. GEORGE WHITEFIELD. 1770.

HAIL, happy ſaint, on thine immortal throne,
Poſſeſt of glory, life, and bliſs unknown;
We hear no more the muſic of thy tongue,
Thy wonted auditories ceaſe to throng.
Thy ſermons in unequall'd accents flow'd,
And ev'ry boſom with devotion glow'd;
Thou didſt in ſtrains of eloquence refin'd
Inflame the heart, and captivate the mind.
Unhappy we the ſetting ſun deplore,
So glorious once, but ah! it ſhines no more.

Behold the prophet in his tow'ring flight!
He leaves the earth for heav'n's unmeaſur'd height,
And worlds unknown receive him from our ſight.
There *Whitefield* wings with rapid courſe his way,
And ſails to *Zion* through vaſt ſeas of day.
Thy pray'rs, great ſaint, and thine inceſſant cries
Have pierc'd the boſom of thy native ſkies.

Thou

This is a published copy of the George Whitefield poem.

George Whitefield

Phillis wrote about other current events, too. The Wheatley family lived in a large house on King Street in Boston, Massachusetts. This street was right in the middle of the city. There was always a lot going on around Phillis.

This was a difficult time for the people who lived in the colonies. British rulers kept passing laws that took freedoms away from colonists. People felt that this was unfair. Many colonists wanted **independence** from Great Britain and the king.

King Street in Boston near the Wheatley's home

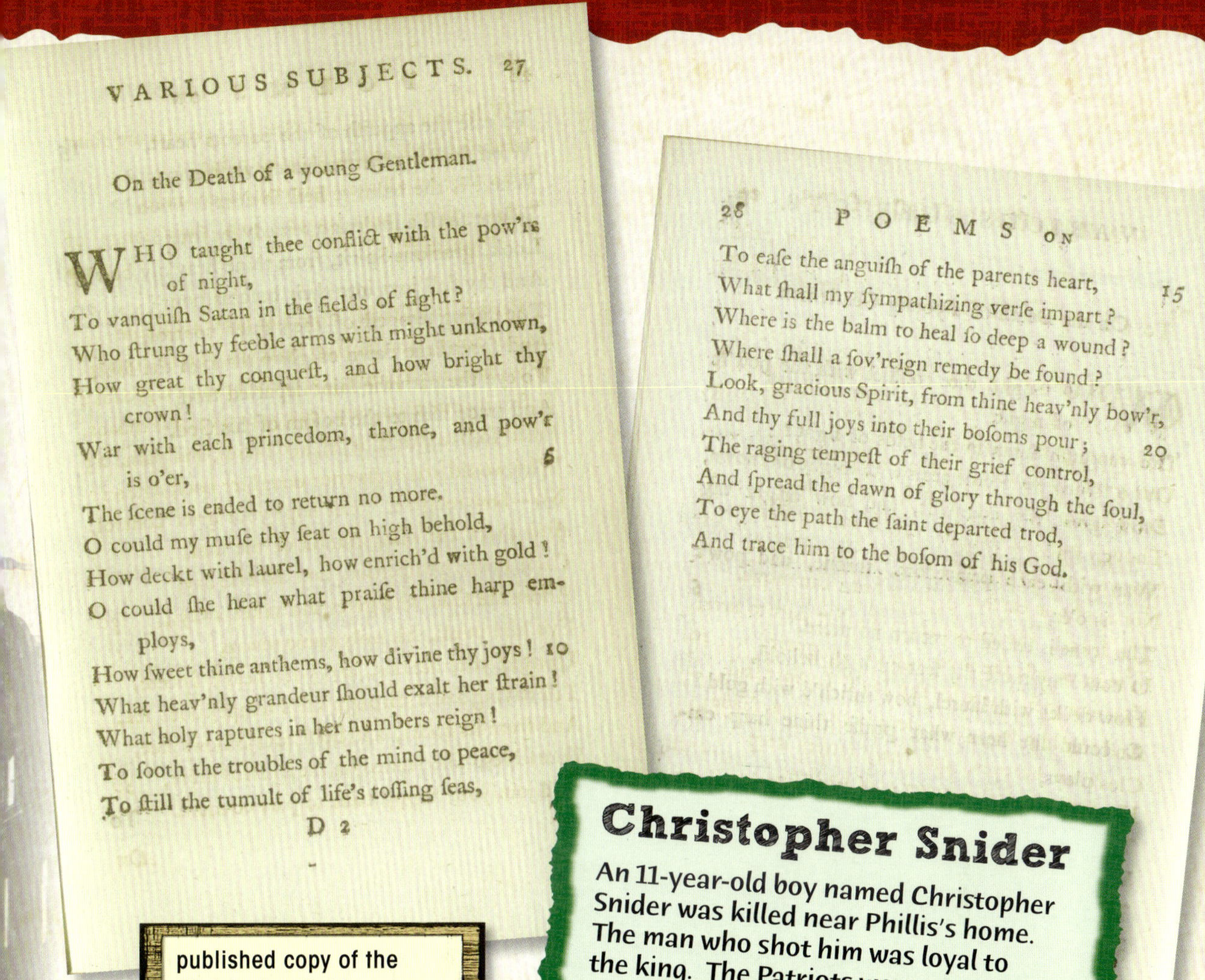

VARIOUS SUBJECTS. 27

On the Death of a young Gentleman.

WHO taught thee conflict with the pow'rs of night,
To vanquiſh Satan in the fields of fight?
Who ſtrung thy feeble arms with might unknown,
How great thy conqueſt, and how bright thy crown!
War with each princedom, throne, and pow'r is o'er,
The ſcene is ended to return no more.
O could my muſe thy ſeat on high behold,
How deckt with laurel, how enrich'd with gold!
O could ſhe hear what praiſe thine harp employs,
How ſweet thine anthems, how divine thy joys!
What heav'nly grandeur ſhould exalt her ſtrain!
What holy raptures in her numbers reign!
To ſooth the troubles of the mind to peace,
To ſtill the tumult of life's toſſing ſeas,

D 2

28 POEMS ON

To eaſe the anguiſh of the parents heart,
What ſhall my ſympathizing verſe impart?
Where is the balm to heal ſo deep a wound?
Where ſhall a ſov'reign remedy be found?
Look, gracious Spirit, from thine heav'nly bow'r,
And thy full joys into their boſoms pour;
The raging tempeſt of their grief control,
And ſpread the dawn of glory through the ſoul,
To eye the path the ſaint departed trod,
And trace him to the boſom of his God.

published copy of the Christopher Snider poem

Christopher Snider

An 11-year-old boy named Christopher Snider was killed near Phillis's home. The man who shot him was loyal to the king. The Patriots were very upset about the boy's death. In a poem, Phillis agreed with the Patriots and wrote how terrible the event was.

Men called **Patriots** started to **protest** the king's actions. The Patriots were based in Boston near Phillis.

Phillis wrote poems about the events in her city. One poem was about an ex-slave named Crispus Attucks. He was shot during the Boston Massacre (MAH-suh-ker). Phillis also wrote about British troops who moved into Boston.

tea party in colonial New England

Phillis's poems were sometimes published in newspapers. People enjoyed reading them. But Mrs. Wheatley wanted to make Phillis more popular in Boston. So, Mrs. Wheatley brought Phillis with her to social events. Phillis was invited to read her poetry aloud.

However, Phillis was usually uncomfortable once she finished her poetry readings. The society women would all sit together to have tea. Most of the time, Phillis chose to sit at a separate table. She did not feel welcome to sit with the white women.

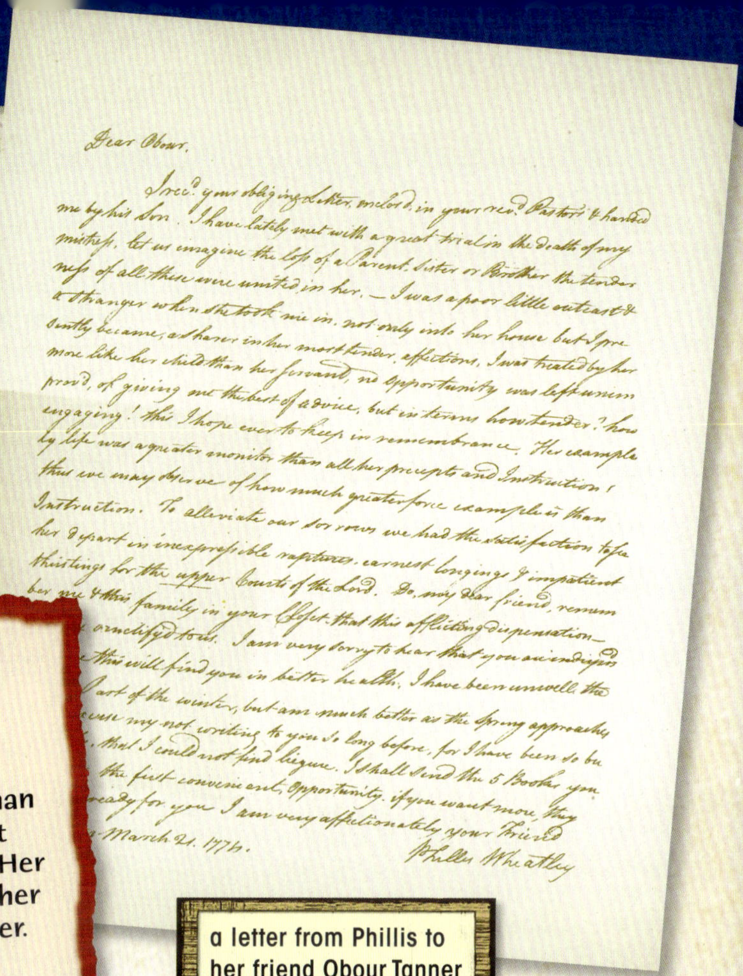

Dear Obour.

I rec.d your obliging Letter, enclos.d in your rev.d Pastor's & handed me by his Son. I have lately met with a great trial in the death of my mistress, let us imagine the loss of a Parent, Sister or Brother the tenderness of all these were united in her. — I was a poor little outcast & a Stranger when she took me in: not only into her house but I presently became a sharer in her most tender affections. I was treated by her more like her child than her Servant, no opportunity was left unimprov.d, of giving me the best of advice, but in terms how tender! how engaging! this I hope ever to keep in remembrance. Her example by life was a greater monitor than all her precepts and Instruction, thus we may observe of how much greater force example is than Instruction. To alleviate our sorrows we had the satisfaction to see her depart in inexpressible raptures, earnest longings & impatient thirstings for the upper Courts of the Lord. Do, my dear friend, remember me & this family in your Closet, that this afflicting dispensation may be sanctified to us. I am very sorry to hear that you are indisposed ... this will find you in better health. I have been unwell the ... part of the winter, but am much better as the Spring approaches ... excuse my not writing to you so long before, for I have been so bu... that I could not find leisure. I shall send the 5 Books you ... the first convenient, Opportunity. if you want more, they ... ready for you I am very affectionately your Friend

... March 21. 1774.

Phillis Wheatley

a letter from Phillis to her friend Obour Tanner

Two Worlds

Phillis did not fit in with white society. Since she was treated differently than other slaves, she didn't fit into their society either. Her only real friend was another slave named Obour Tanner. Phillis and Obour wrote letters to each other for many years.

One day, Phillis went with Mrs. Wheatley to a friend's home. When she arrived, Phillis was introduced to Mrs. Fitch. Mrs. Fitch's husband owned a ship called *Phillis*. It turned out that he was the man who had brought Phillis to Boston! Everyone was a bit uncomfortable that afternoon.

By 1772, Susannah Wheatley thought that someone should publish a book of Phillis's poems. The poems that had been printed in newspapers were very popular. People enjoyed reading Phillis's work in the colonies and in England.

It was hard for Phillis to get her work published because she was a slave. Mrs. Wheatley tried to find a colonial publisher. It was very expensive to print books at that time. No one wanted to risk losing money on a slave's book.

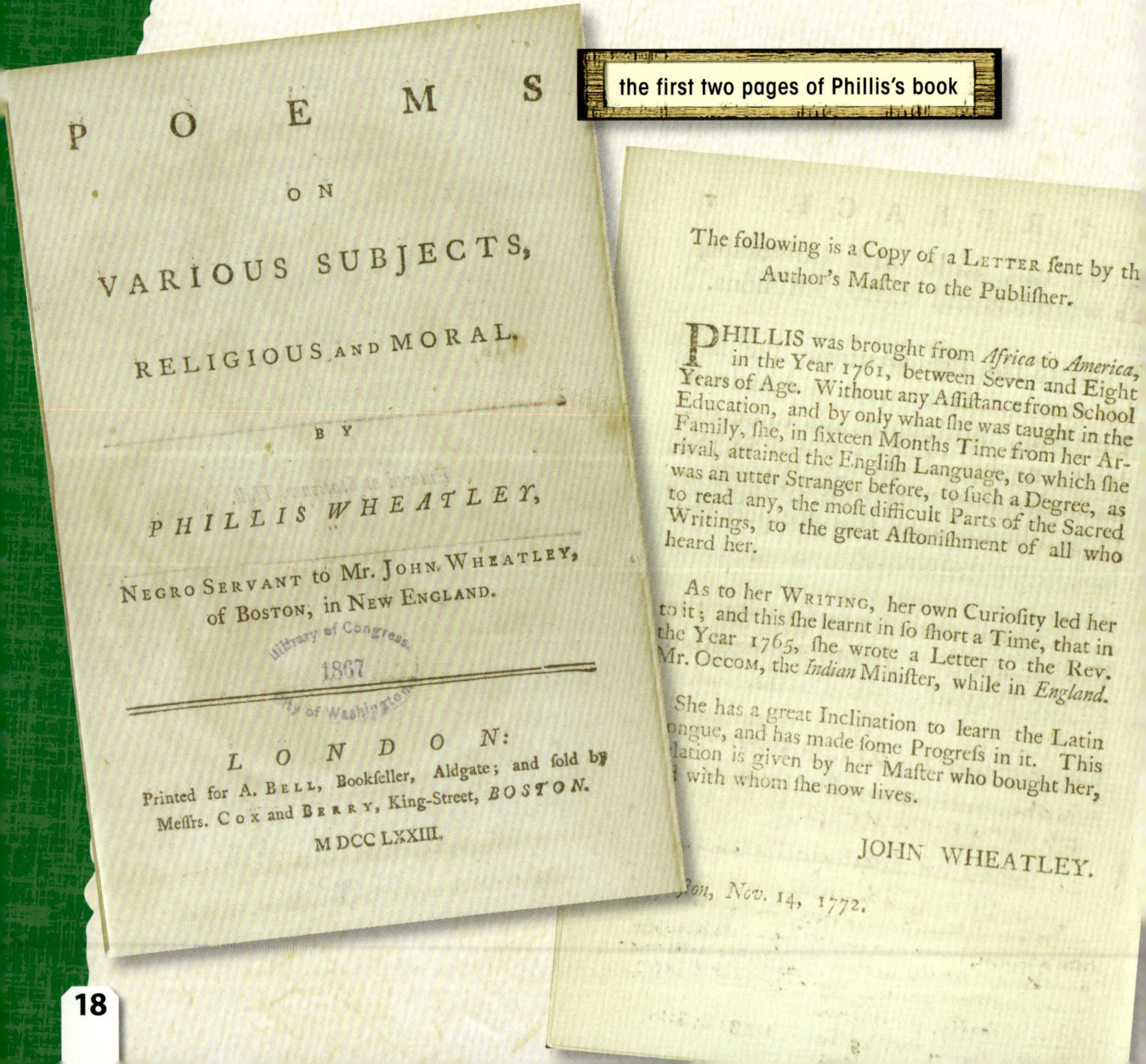

P O E M S

ON

VARIOUS SUBJECTS,

RELIGIOUS AND MORAL.

BY

PHILLIS WHEATLEY,

NEGRO SERVANT to Mr. JOHN WHEATLEY, of BOSTON, in NEW ENGLAND.

LONDON:

Printed for A. BELL, Bookſeller, Aldgate; and ſold by Meſſrs. COX and BERRY, King-Street, BOSTON.

MDCCLXXIII.

The following is a Copy of a LETTER ſent by th Author's Maſter to the Publiſher.

PHILLIS was brought from *Africa* to *America*, in the Year 1761, between Seven and Eight Years of Age. Without any Aſſiſtance from School Education, and by only what ſhe was taught in the Family, ſhe, in ſixteen Months Time from her Arrival, attained the Engliſh Language, to which ſhe was an utter Stranger before, to ſuch a Degree, as to read any, the moſt difficult Parts of the Sacred Writings, to the great Aſtoniſhment of all who heard her.

As to her WRITING, her own Curioſity led her to it; and this ſhe learnt in ſo ſhort a Time, that in the Year 1765, ſhe wrote a Letter to the Rev. Mr. OCCOM, the *Indian* Miniſter, while in *England*.

She has a great Inclination to learn the Latin ...ongue, and has made ſome Progreſs in it. This ...lation is given by her Maſter who bought her, ... with whom ſhe now lives.

JOHN WHEATLEY.

...ſton, Nov. 14, 1772.

the first two pages of Phillis's book

So, Mrs. Wheatley found someone in England to print the book. At first, the printer did not want to publish the book. He did not believe that a slave could have written so beautifully. Some important men from Boston told him that Phillis was a gifted poet. After that, the publisher agreed to print the book.

colonial printing press

THE
TENTH MUSE
Lately ſprung up in AMERICA.
OR
Severall Poems, compiled
with great variety of VVit
and Learning, full of delight.
Wherein eſpecially is contained a com-
pleat diſcourſe and deſcription of
The Four Elements,

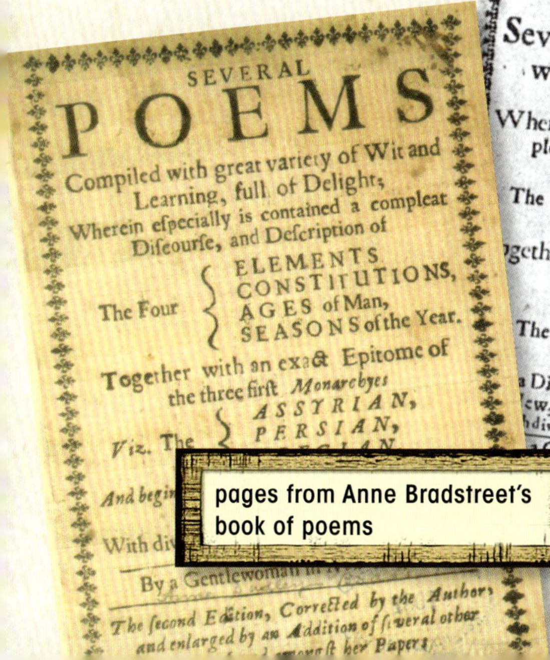

SEVERAL
POEMS
Compiled with great variety of Wit and
Learning, full of Delight;
Wherein eſpecially is contained a compleat
Diſcourſe, and Deſcription of
The Four { ELEMENTS, CONSTITUTIONS, AGES of Man, SEASONS of the Year.
Together with an exact Epitome of
the three firſt Monarchyes
Viz. The { ASSYRIAN, PERSIAN,
By a Gentlewoman
The ſecond Edition, Corrected by the Author,
and enlarged by an Addition of ſeveral other

pages from Anne Bradstreet's book of poems

Black Woman Poet

Phillis's book was the first book published by a black woman in America. She was only the second woman in America to have a book published. Anne Bradstreet was the first. In 1650, Bradstreet published a book of poems.

To England and Back

In May 1773, Nathaniel Wheatley took Phillis to England. She was supposed to meet the **Countess** of Huntingdon. The countess helped pay for the publication of Phillis's book. She decided that the book should have Phillis's picture on the first page. That image is the only known picture of Phillis created during her lifetime.

Phillis enjoyed her visit to England. She got to meet many people who had read her poetry. She was treated better in England than she was in the colonies. Finally, the countess sent an invitation to Phillis. She invited Phillis and Nathaniel to come to her country house.

Unfortunately, Phillis received some bad news. Mrs. Wheatley was very sick. She wrote and asked Phillis to come home. Phillis never got to meet the countess. She had to leave England before her book was published.

This painting of Phillis Wheatley was created after she died.

Countess of Huntingdon

the dedication page from Phillis's book

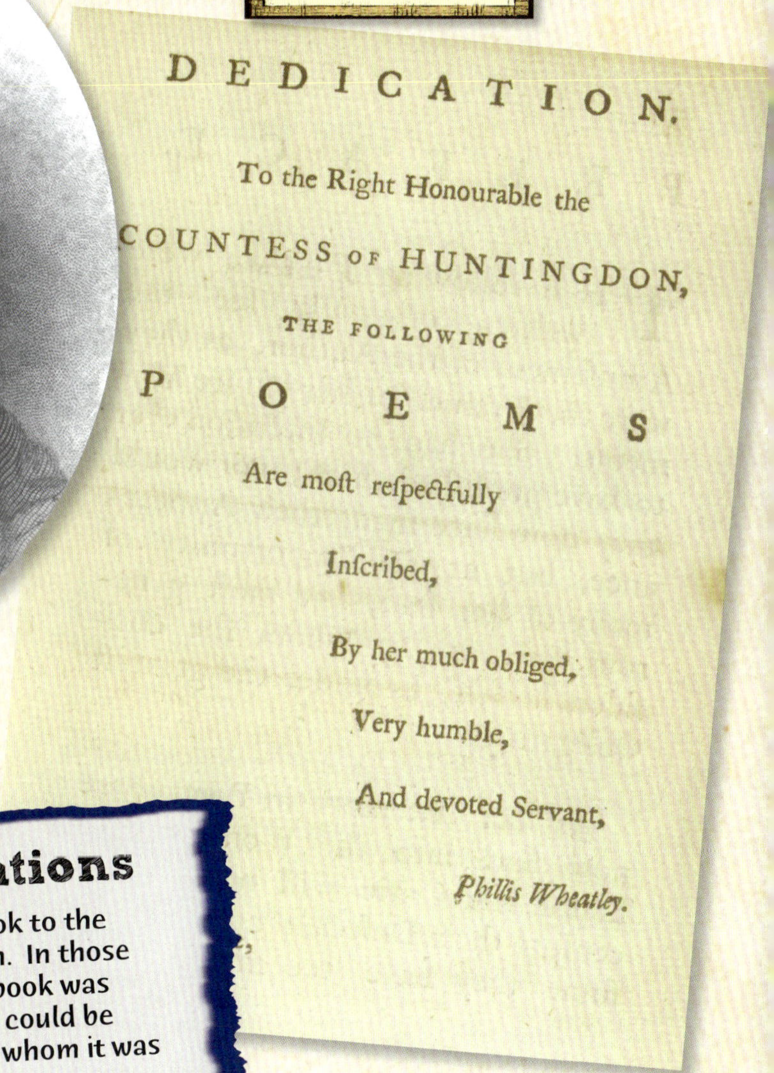

DEDICATION.

To the Right Honourable the

COUNTESS OF HUNTINGDON,

THE FOLLOWING

POEMS

Are moſt reſpectfully

Inſcribed,

By her much obliged,

Very humble,

And devoted Servant,

Phillis Wheatley.

Book Dedications

Phillis dedicated her book to the Countess of Huntingdon. In those days, a **dedication** of a book was very important. A book could be popular just because of whom it was dedicated to.

Phillis arrived home to find more problems between the British and the colonists. Dressed as American Indians, Patriots boarded a British ship at night. They threw boxes of tea into the harbor to protest British laws. This happened just a few blocks from Phillis's house on King Street. Her published book was supposed to arrive in the same harbor any day.

To the Rescue

The British prevented supplies from arriving in Boston Harbor. They wanted to starve the Patriots to make them behave. So, the other colonies secretly sent food to help Boston.

The British acted quickly. They closed Boston Harbor until the colonists paid for the damages. They stationed more troops in Boston and limited their right to assemble. Phillis had to wait a little longer to receive her book.

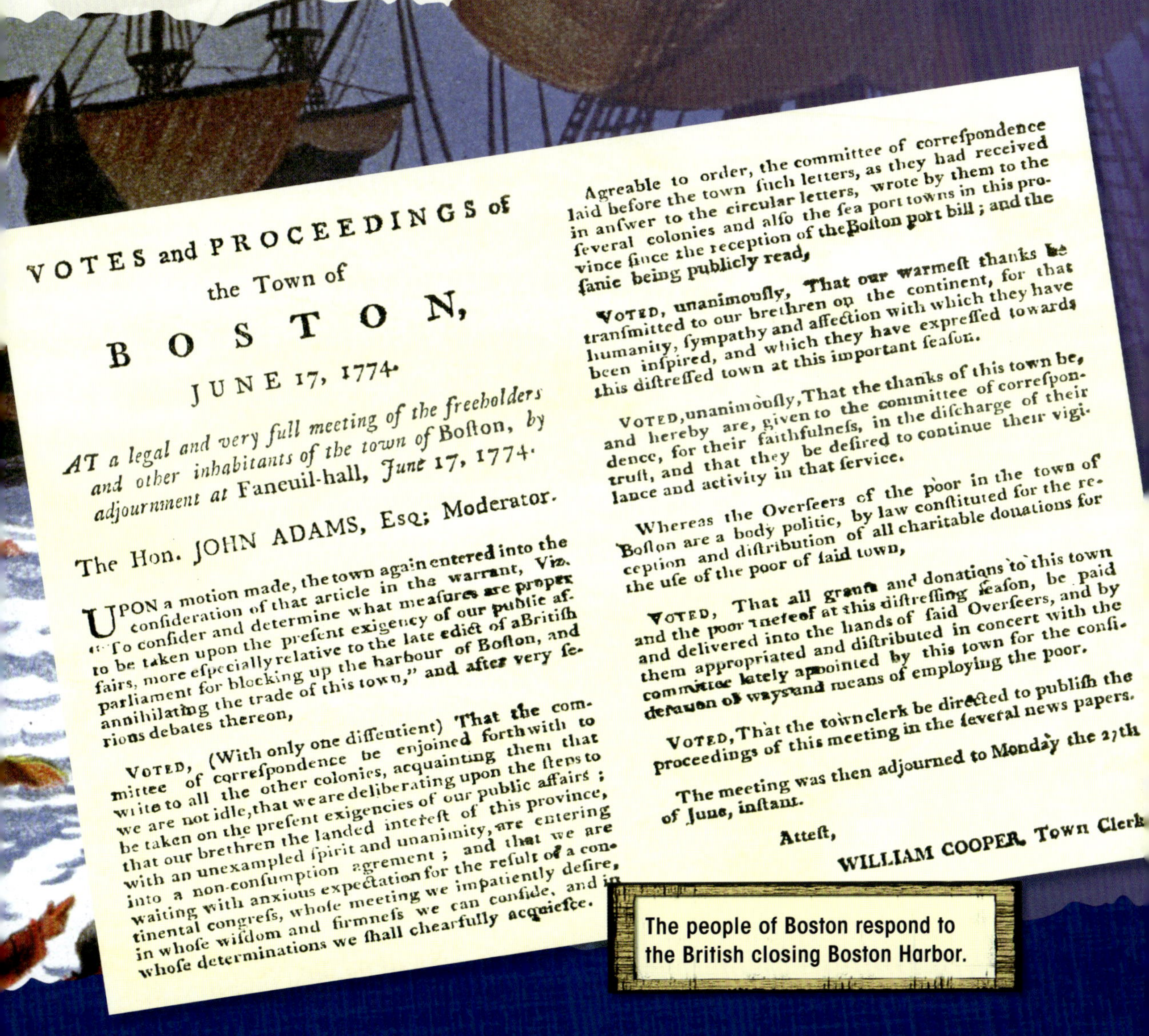

VOTES and PROCEEDINGS of
the Town of
BOSTON,
JUNE 17, 1774.

AT a legal and very full meeting of the freeholders and other inhabitants of the town of Boſton, *by adjournment at* Faneuil-hall, *June* 17, 1774.

The Hon. JOHN ADAMS, Esq; Moderator.

UPON a motion made, the town again entered into the conſideration of that article in the warrant, Viz. "To conſider and determine what meaſures are proper to be taken upon the preſent exigency of our public affairs, more eſpecially relative to the late edict of a Britiſh parliament for blocking up the harbour of Boſton, and annihilating the trade of this town," and after very ſerious debates thereon,

VOTED, (With only one diſſentient) That the committee of correſpondence be enjoined forthwith to write to all the other colonies, acquainting them that we are not idle, that we are deliberating upon the ſteps to be taken on the preſent exigencies of our public affairs; that our brethren the landed intereſt of this province, with an unexampled ſpirit and unanimity, are entering into a non-conſumption agrement; and that we are waiting with anxious expectation for the reſult of a continental congreſs, whoſe meeting we impatiently deſire, in whoſe wiſdom and firmneſs we can confide, and in whoſe determinations we ſhall chearfully acquieſce.

Agreable to order, the committee of correſpondence laid before the town ſuch letters, as they had received in anſwer to the circular letters, wrote by them to the ſeveral colonies and alſo the ſea port towns in this province ſince the reception of the Boſton port bill; and the ſame being publicly read,

VOTED, unanimouſly, That our warmeſt thanks be tranſmitted to our brethren on the continent, for that humanity, ſympathy and affection with which they have been inſpired, and which they have expreſſed towards this diſtreſſed town at this important ſeaſon.

VOTED, unanimouſly, That the thanks of this town be, and hereby are, given to the committee of correſpondence, for their faithfulneſs, in the diſcharge of their truſt, and that they be deſired to continue their vigilance and activity in that ſervice.

Whereas the Overſeers of the poor in the town of Boſton are a body politic, by law conſtituted for the reception and diſtribution of all charitable donations for the uſe of the poor of ſaid town,

VOTED, That all grants and donations to this town and the poor thereof at this diſtreſſing ſeaſon, be paid and delivered into the hands of ſaid Overſeers, and by them appropriated and diſtributed in concert with the committee lately appointed by this town for the conſideration of ways and means of employing the poor.

VOTED, That the town clerk be directed to publiſh the proceedings of this meeting in the ſeveral news papers.

The meeting was then adjourned to Monday the 27th of June, inſtant.

Atteſt,

WILLIAM COOPER, Town Clerk

The people of Boston respond to the British closing Boston Harbor.

Freedom at Last!

In 1773, Mr. Wheatley freed Phillis. Slaves could be freed in a couple different ways. They could buy their freedom. But this was very difficult since most slaves couldn't earn money. Their owners could also give slaves their freedom. This is what Mr. Wheatley did for Phillis.

Phillis was no longer a slave. But, she continued to live with the Wheatleys. Mrs. Wheatley was very ill and Phillis helped take care of her.

In March 1774, Susannah Wheatley died. Losing Mrs. Wheatley was difficult for Phillis. Phillis had grown close to Mrs. Wheatley over the years.

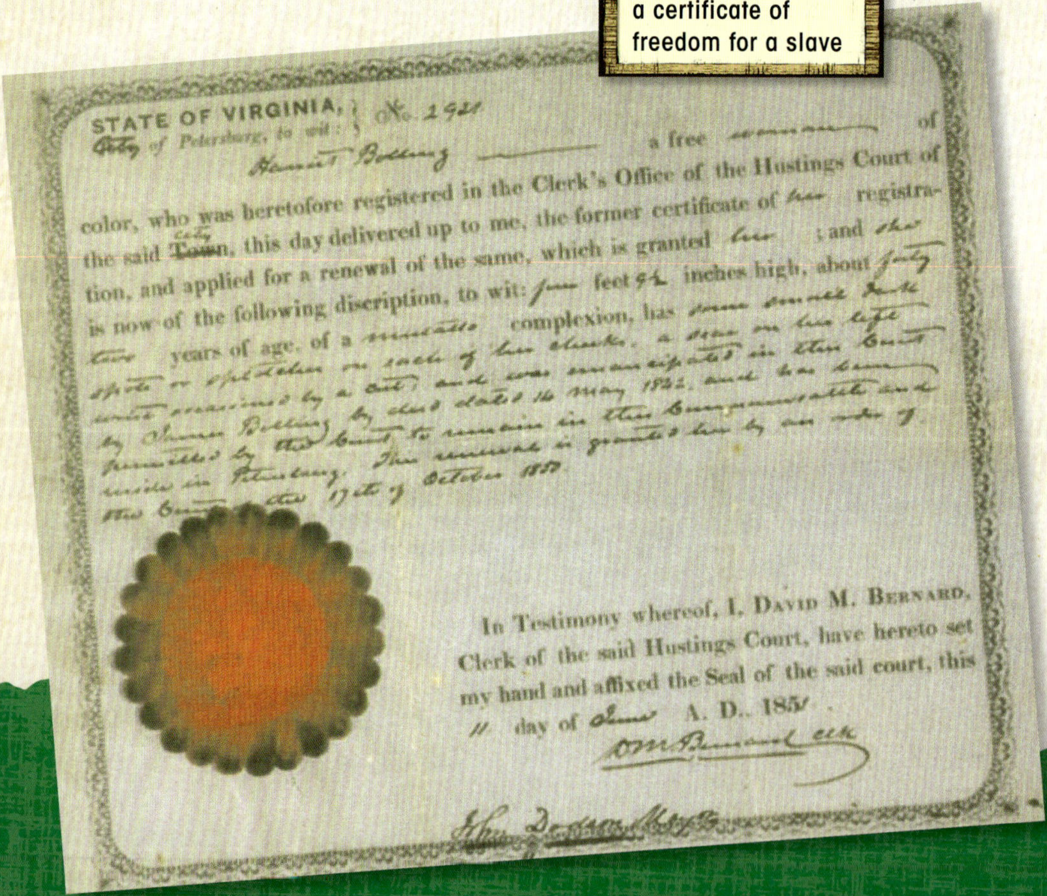

STATE OF VIRGINIA, City of Petersburg, to wit: No. 2921

Harriet Bolling a free woman of color, who was heretofore registered in the Clerk's Office of the Hustings Court of the said City, this day delivered up to me, the former certificate of her registration, and applied for a renewal of the same, which is granted her ; and she is now of the following discription, to wit: five feet 9½ inches high, about forty two years of age, of a mulatto complexion, has [illegible]

In Testimony whereof, I, David M. Bernard, Clerk of the said Hustings Court, have hereto set my hand and affixed the Seal of the said court, this 11 day of June A. D. 1851 .

[illegible]

a certificate of freedom for a slave

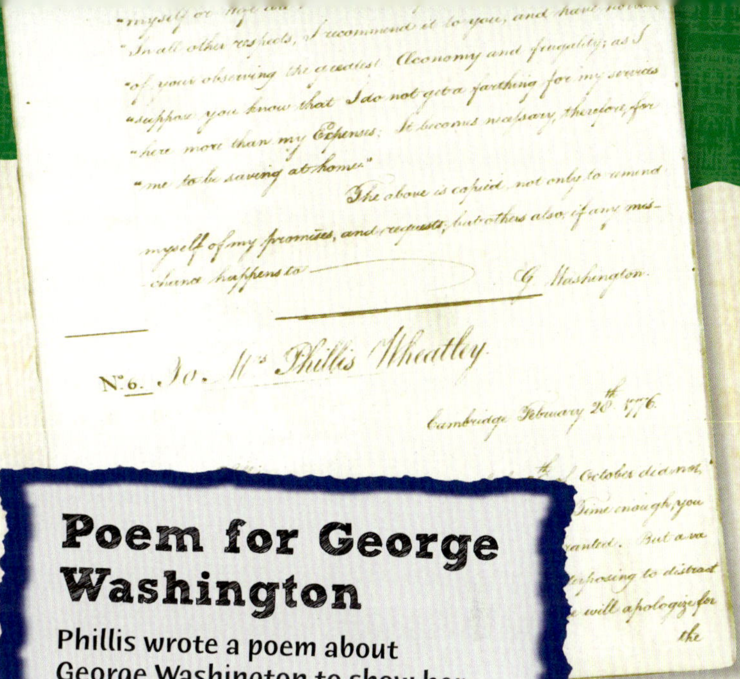
"In all other respects, I recommend it to you, and have no doubt
"of your observing the greatest Economy and frugality; as I
"suppose you know that I do not get a farthing for my services
"here more than my Expenses; It becomes necessary, therefore, for
"me to be saving at home."
The above is copied not only to remind
myself of my promises, and requests; but others also, if any mis-
chance happens to —— G Washington.

No. 6. To Mrs Phillis Wheatley.
Cambridge February 28th 1776.

Poem for George Washington

Phillis wrote a poem about George Washington to show her support for the Continental army. Washington was very impressed with the poem. In February 1776, Phillis traveled to Washington's camp to meet him.

General George Washington

Phillis had to earn money now that she was a free woman. She tried to sell her book in the colonies. The publisher in England sent her 300 copies. She placed advertisements in newspapers. Her books sold quickly.

Then, the American Revolution started. Ships from England could not bring her books to the colonies anymore.

"Liberty and Peace"

In 1778, Phillis met a man named John Peters. He was a free black man who lived in Boston. Soon, they married. John worked very hard and they had a nice house. Unfortunately, the war years were hard. John lost his job and had a hard time making money.

Phillis continued to write during this time. But, she never published another book. So, she was not making much money either. All three of John and Phillis's children died young. Phillis died in December 1784. She was only 31 years old.

The last poem that Phillis wrote was called "Liberty and Peace." During her life in America, Phillis saw a lot of violence. By 1784, the country had finished a war. People were working together to build a new nation. This poem describes the **patriotism** felt throughout the states. As always, Phillis wrote with great emotion. Her words describe an exciting time in the country's history. People today are lucky to have Phillis's poems about the past.

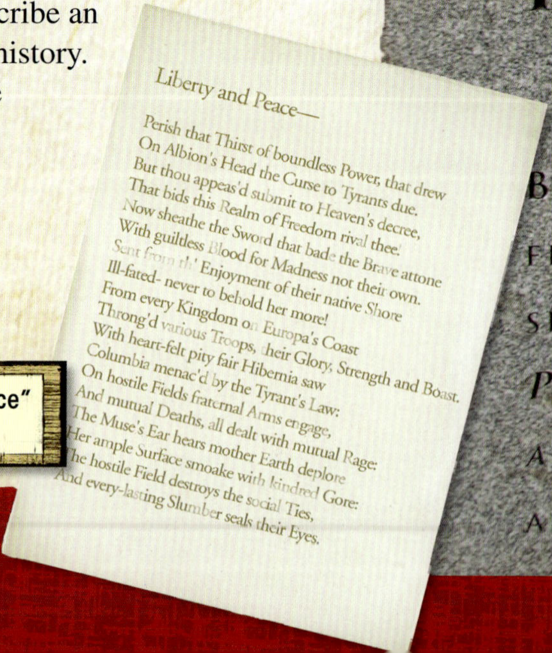

Liberty and Peace—

Perish that Thirst of boundless Power, that drew
On Albion's Head the Curse to Tyrants due.
But thou appeas'd submit to Heaven's decree,
That bids this Realm of Freedom rival thee!
Now sheathe the Sword that bade the Brave attone
With guiltless Blood for Madness not their own.
Sent from th' Enjoyment of their native Shore
Ill-fated- never to behold her more!
From every Kingdom on Europa's Coast
Throng'd various Troops, their Glory, Strength and Boast.
With heart-felt pity fair Hibernia saw
Columbia menac'd by the Tyrant's Law:
On hostile Fields fraternal Arms engage,
And mutual Deaths, all dealt with mutual Rage:
The Muse's Ear hears mother Earth deplore
Her ample Surface smoake with kindred Gore:
The hostile Field destroys the social Ties,
And every-lasting Slumber seals their Eyes.

part of "Liberty and Peace" by Phillis Wheatley

Wheatley's Will

When Mr. Wheatley died in 1778, he was still a very rich man. His **will** did not mention Phillis. He left no money or property to her. She had served his family for 12 years. Even though they treated her like family, was she really family?

a statue of Phillis in Boston

Describe It!

Phillis Wheatley led an uncommon life for a slave. If she had arrived on a ship in the South, her life would have been quite different.

Find out how life was different for slaves in the South. Then, write a "what if" version of Phillis Wheatley's life in the South. Describe her living conditions, her working conditions, and the attitudes of her owners. Would she have learned to write or not? You decide!

POEMS
ON
VARIOUS SUBJECTS,
RELIGIOUS AND MORAL.
BY
PHILLIS WHEATLEY,
NEGRO SERVANT to Mr. JOHN WHEATLEY,
of BOSTON, in NEW ENGLAND.
Library of Congress
1867
Aldgate; and fold by
BOSTON.

Glossary

captive—a person who is captured and is kept as a prisoner

countess—a rank given to some upper-class British women

dedication—a part at the beginning of a book that names someone who is special to the author

illegal—against the law

independence—the state of not being controlled or ruled by another country

ministers—leaders of the church

patriotism—love for one's country

Patriots—people who supported American independence from Great Britain

plantation—a large farm that produces crops for money

protest—to fight against something

slave—a person who is forced to work without pay and has no freedom

slave merchant—an owner of one of the ships that brought slaves to the colonies

will—a document that describes where someone's money and property go after they die

Index

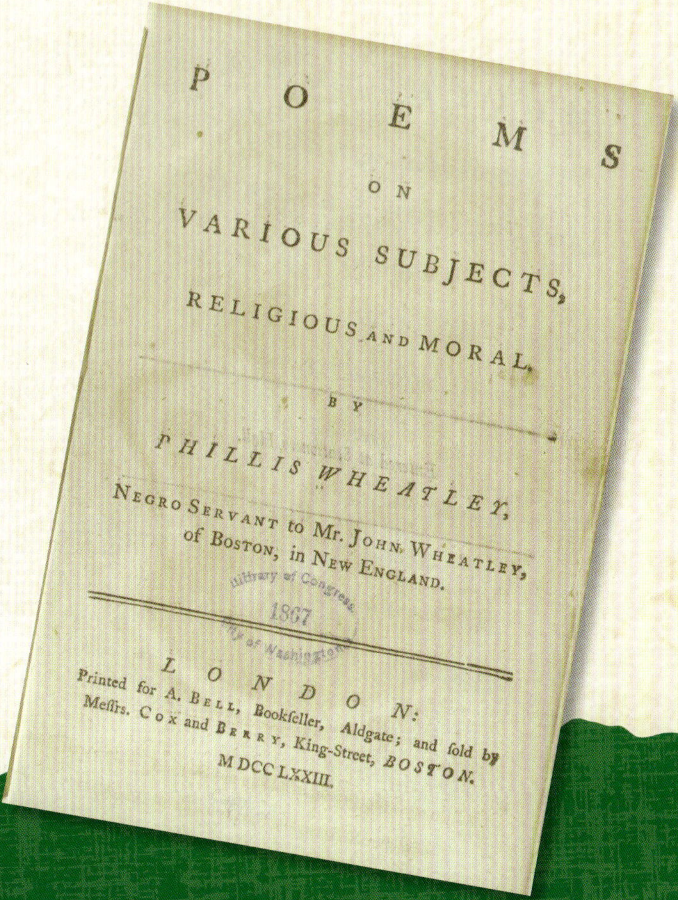

POEMS

ON

VARIOUS SUBJECTS,

RELIGIOUS AND MORAL.

BY

PHILLIS WHEATLEY,

NEGRO SERVANT to Mr. JOHN WHEATLEY, of BOSTON, in NEW ENGLAND.

LONDON:

Printed for A. BELL, Bookseller, Aldgate; and sold by Messrs. COX and BERRY, King-Street, BOSTON.

MDCCLXXIII.

Your Turn!

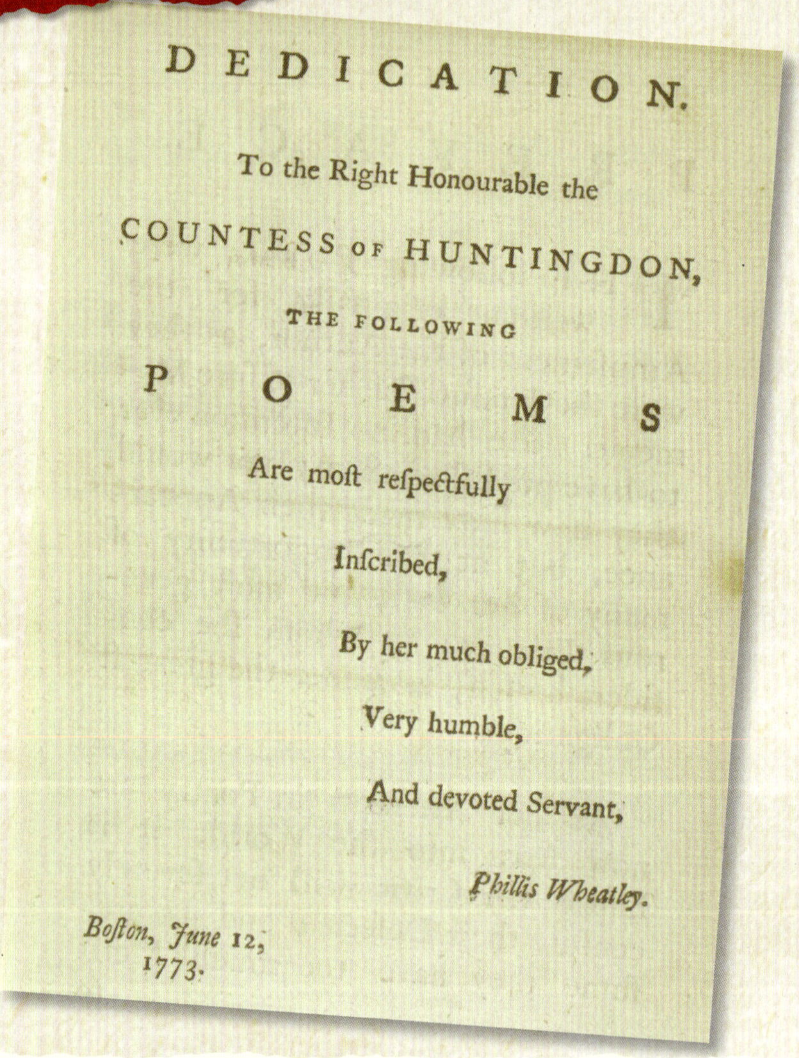

DEDICATION.

To the Right Honourable the

COUNTESS OF HUNTINGDON,

THE FOLLOWING

P O E M S

Are moſt reſpectfully

Inſcribed,

By her much obliged,

Very humble,

And devoted Servant,

Phillis Wheatley.

Boſton, June 12,
1773.

Book Dedication

The Countess of Huntingdon helped pay for the publication of Phillis's book. So, Phillis dedicated her book to the countess. Who else might Phillis have dedicated her book to, if she had the chance? Write a new dedication page and explain why Phillis would dedicate the book to this new person.